Basic Comprehension

Information about the worksheets

Basic Comprehension is a book of 44 worksheets for photocopying, designed primarily to help students whose reading ability is at a fairly basic level to improve their reading and comprehension skills. Many of the worksheets first appeared in *News Worksheet**, in which a basic comprehension worksheet is a regular item. We have compiled this book in order to bring these worksheets, many of them revised and improved, to a wider audience, along with a selection of new worksheets in the same format.

Each worksheet contains a short piece of reading matter followed by a number of exercises. The exercises are arranged in sections, and instructions to students are kept as brief as possible. In most cases, the title of each section gives sufficient explanation as to what is required but, where necessary, an extra sentence or two is added to make things clear. Students should soon become familiar with the format of the worksheets and should find their repetition helpful.

All the exercises are based on the text, and words and phrases from it. They encourage constant re-reading, thinking and checking. Some exercises should be read aloud, especially those in the *Which word is the odd one out?* and spelling sections, in which both the sounds and the meanings of words are taken into consideration. Most of the exercises demand little writing and even those which do could be tackled orally.

Answers are not given because most can be found by referring back to the reading text. In some cases, there is more than one correct answer. The index *(p.48)* gives some guidance as to the topics covered in the worksheets.

Basic Comprehension should prove useful for work related to NVQ Key Skills, National Curriculum (English) and City & Guilds & SCOTVEC Wordpower Certificates.

*News Worksheet is a topical set of exercises (10 x A4 pages) for practising reading, writing, spelling and maths. It has been published 3 times a year since 1988. News Worksheet is only available directly from Brown and Brown. If you do not already subscribe to it and would like further details, please contact Brown and Brown at the address given overleaf.

Please read the copyright / photocopying restrictions below.

Publishers: Brown and Brown,
                Keeper's Cottage,
                Westward,
                Wigton
                Cumbria CA7 8NQ
                Tel. 016973 42915

Copyright   © Hugh and Margaret Brown 1999

If you would like to receive our catalogue of publications for teaching reading, spelling, writing and basic maths, please contact:

Brown and Brown Publishing, Keeper's Cottage, Westward, Wigton, Cumbria CA7 8NQ
Tel. 016973 42915

First published 1999

ISBN 1 870596 70 6

Printed by Reed's Ltd., Penrith, Cumbria on Corona 100% recycled paper and card.

Contents

*The worksheets (**pp. 4-33**) were first published in the **News Worksheet** from Spring 1988 to Autumn 1998. They are arranged in order of the date they appeared and the date is printed after the reading text on each worksheet. For this book, many of the worksheets have been revised in both text and layout.*

*The worksheets (**pp. 34-47**) were written for this book in Spring 1999 and are not dated in the text.*

Keep warm in winter

Old people need to keep warm in winter. The old are more at risk than others. When it is very cold, keep one room warm, at about 70°F. Wear a lot of thin clothes. This is better than a few thick clothes. About one fifth of the body's heat is lost from the head, so it is a good idea to wear a hat indoors and in bed. Drink a lot of hot drinks and eat plenty of food, including sweets and chocolate.

Spring 1988

A. Yes or No ?

1. Is it a good idea to wear a hat in bed if it is cold ?

2. In the cold, should you wear a few thick clothes ?

3. Must old people keep warm when it is cold ?

4. Is 70°F a warm room ?

5. Should you drink a lot of hot drinks ?

B. Fill in the right word

1. Old people need to keep _____ .
   (worm / warn / warm)

2. The old are _____ at risk.
   (mare / more / moor)

3. Eat plenty of _____ .
   (foot / fond / food)

4. One fifth of the body's heat is lost from the _____ .
   (heat / head / hear)

5. Wear a hat in _____ .
   (beb / deb / bed)

C. Sort out these jumbled words

lod	wram
dogo	krind
doof	taubo
hade	triwen
dolc	hint

D. Fill in the missing word

1. It is a good idea to wear a indoors.

2. When it is very keep one room warm.

3. Old people need keep warm in winter.

4. The are more at risk than others.

5. Wear a lot thin clothes.

E. True / False / Maybe

1. Old people are not at risk in the cold.

2. Thick clothes keep you warm.

3. A lot of heat is lost from the head.

4. Sweets and chocolates are good for you.

5. Cold drinks are bad for you.

F. Opposites

Find a word in the article which means the opposite of each of these:

young	many
cold	worse
found	bad

Hijack over

On a flight from Bangkok to Kuwait on April 5th 1988, an aeroplane was hijacked and forced to land in Iran. After 3 days, most of the women and all of the Western passengers were released. The plane then flew to Cyprus. Two hostages were killed and 13 others were freed.

A few days later, the plane flew on to Algiers. After 8 days of deadlock the hijack ended. The 31 hostages and crew of Flight KU 422 were released. The hijackers were allowed to go free.

Summer 1988

A. Yes or No ?

1. Was the flight going to Kuwait ?
2. Were all the women released in Iran ?
3. Did the plane land in 3 countries ?
4. Was the plane hijacked in Bangkok ?
5. Were there 31 hostages altogether ?

B. Fill in the right word

1. The plane then _____ to Cyprus.
   (flow / flew / flaw)
2. Two hostages _____ killed.
   (were / wear / where)
3. The hijack ended _____ 8 days.
   (often / alter / after)
4. 13 hostages were _____ in Cyprus.
   (free / fred / freed)
5. The hijackers were _____ to go free.
   (aloud / allow / allowed)

C. Fill in the missing word

1. All of Western passengers were released.
2. The then flew to Cyprus.
3. A few later, the plane flew on to Algiers.
4. After 8 days of the hijack ended.
5. The hijackers were allowed to free.

D. Which word is the odd one out ?

1. hijackers   hostages   plane   crew
2. women   days   plane   passengers
3. freed   released   killed   flew
4. Algiers   was   after   allowed
5. Iran   Bangkok   April   Cyprus

E. True / False / Maybe

1. All the Western passengers were freed in Iran.
2. 13 passengers were killed in Cyprus.
3. The plane spent 5 days in Cyprus.
4. None of the hijackers was killed.
5. The hijack ended on April 21st.

F. Sort out these jumbled words

sady   prAli   welf

mowen   rewe   rewc

reef   wiKuta   nalep

G. What do you think ?

1. Should the hijackers have been freed ?
2. Should Governments ever do deals with hijackers ?

Raw sewage in harbour

In Portsmouth, yesterday, 5 million gallons of raw sewage were put into the harbour by council workers. Earlier in the week, leaks had been found in the main sewage pipe. The council had to put the sewage into the harbour so that they could do repairs on the pipe.

Swimmers and sailors were told to keep clear of the harbour. But the city engineer said, "The sewage is not a health hazard."

Autumn 1988

A. Yes or No ?

1. Did council workers put sewage into the harbour ?
2. Was the main sewage pipe leaking ?
3. Did the city engineer say that sewage is a health hazard ?
4. Were swimmers warned about the sewage ?
5. Is Portsmouth by the sea ?

B. Fill in the missing word

1. 5 million gallons of raw were put into the harbour.
2. The council had put the sewage into the harbour.
3. Earlier the week, leaks had been found.
4. Swimmers and sailors were to keep clear of the harbour.
5. The sewage is a health hazard.

C. Fill in the missing letters

The same 2 letters are missing from each pair of words. Fill them in.

1. w _ _ k   k _ _ p
2. c _ _ ncil   f _ _ nd
3. l _ _ k   cl _ _ r
4. mi _ _ ions   ga _ _ ons
5. swimm _ _ s   work _ _ s

D. Fill in the right word

1. 5 million gallons of _____ sewage were put into the harbour.
   (row / war / raw)
2. Leaks had been found in the _____ sewage pipe.
   (mane / man / main)
3. The council did repairs on the _____ .
   (pile / pipe / pine)
4. Swimmers were _____ to keep clear.
   (toll / told / tolled)
5. Sewage is _____ a health hazard.
   (not / now / no)

E. True / False / Maybe

1. Raw sewage was put into Plymouth harbour.
2. Leaks were found in the main waste pipe.
3. There were boats in the harbour.
4. Workers were told to keep clear of the harbour.
5. Sewage is not a health hazard.

M1 Air Crash

On Sunday, January 8th 1989, a plane flying from London to Belfast tried to land at East Midlands Airport. One engine was on fire. The plane should have been able to fly on the other one, but the wrong engine was shut down. The plane crashed by the side of the M1.

44 people were killed in the crash. Some newspapers called the pilot a hero one day and then blamed him the next day. Later, it was found that the plane had a fault and the pilot was not to blame.

Spring 1989

A. Fill in the right word

1. The plane should _____ been able to fly on one engine.   *(had / have / of)*
2. 44 people were killed in the _____ .   *(cash / crush / crash)*
3. The wrong engine was shut _____ .   *(down / dawn / drown)*
4. The plane crashed by the _____ of the M1.   *(site / said / side)*
5. One engine was on _____ .   *(fir / fair / fire)*

B. Fill in the missing word

1. The plane tried to land at Midlands Airport.
2. One engine was fire.
3. The wrong engine was down.
4. 44 people were killed in the.
5. The plane crashed by the of the M1.

C. True / False / Don't know

1. The plane was flying from Belfast to London.
2. The plane could fly on one engine.
3. Both engines were on fire.
4. The plane crashed on the M1.
5. The pilot was a hero.

D. Answer these questions

1. Where was the plane going to ?
2. Why did the plane try to land at East Midlands Airport ?
3. Why did the plane crash ?
4. Who was to blame for the crash ?

Couple refuse to ring changes

British Telecom engineers got a shock when they went to move a telephone from a farmhouse in Lincolnshire in 1989. They found that the 'phone was a 1930 candlestick model, worth £400. It had been in use since 1931. The owners, Mr. and Mrs. Evans, wanted it moved to their new retirement bungalow in a nearby village.

British Telecom said that they did not normally reconnect old 'phones but, in this case, they agreed to do so. It is thought to be the only one of that kind still working in the United Kingdom.

Summer 1989

A. True / False / Maybe

1. BT agreed to reconnect the 'phone.
2. The 'phone was made in 1930.
3. The 'phone cost Mr. and Mrs. Evans £400 in 1931.
4. The owners of the farmhouse were Mr. and Mrs. Evans.
5. The farmhouse is in Lincolnshire.
6. Mr. and Mrs. Evans were moving to a new bungalow.
7. The bungalow is in Lincolnshire
8. The 'phone had been in use for 58 years.

B. Fill in the missing word

1. The 'phone was 1930 candlestick model.
2. They agreed to so.
3. Mr. and Evans wanted it moved.
4. British engineers got a shock.
5. Had been in use since 1931.

C. Complete these words *(from the article)*

farm _ _ _ _ _   normal _ _   engine _ _ _

candle _ _ _ _ _   bung _ _ _ _   tele _ _ _ _ _

D. Abbreviations
Which words in the article are these short for ?

'phone   U.K.   Lincs.   B.T.   didn't   it's

Slow note from China

In China, in 1939, Mark Earl wrote to his church in London to ask if he could get married and if his bride-to-be could go out to China. The letter did not arrive, but the girl went to China in 1940 and they got married. This year will be their golden wedding. They now live in England and the letter has just been delivered by Royal Mail - 50 years too late !

The letter had been stopped by the Germans in 1939 and, after the war, it was sent to the U.S.A. A few weeks ago it was sent back to Germany and then to England. The letter was marked *VIA QUICKEST ROUTE*.

Spring 1990

A. Fill in the right word

1. The girl _____ to China in 1940.   *(want / went / when)*
2. They _____ live in England.   *(know / no / now)*
3. A few weeks ago it was sent _____ to Germany.   *(back / bank / bark)*
4. The letter has just _____ delivered.   *(be / bean / been)*
5. _____ the war it was sent to the U.S.A.   *(Afar / Often / After)*

B. Fill in the missing letter

marr__ed   y__ars   g__lden

arri__e   co__ld   de__ivered

C. Fill in the missing word

1. Mark Earl wrote his church in London.
2. The letter had been stopped the Germans.
3. The letter not arrive.
4. They now live England.
5. After the war, it sent to the U.S.A.

D. True / False / Don't know

1. The letter arrived 50 years too late.
2. They got married in 1940.
3. The letter went to the U.S.A. in 1941.
4. Mr. and Mrs. Earl came back to England in 1946.
5. The word *via* means *by way of*.

A bit much !

A Scottish girl who moved to the U.S.A. last year has been sent a final Poll Tax demand. Strathclyde Regional Council sent her a second letter telling her she had 7 days to pay or they would take her to court. The amount that she owes them is 28 pence and so far the Council has spent £1 in stamps for the two letters.

When her sister rang the Council they said that, as the Poll Tax demand was for less than £2, they would write it off. Couldn't they have decided that a bit sooner ?

Summer 1990

A. True / False / Maybe

1. The girl had 28 days to pay.
2. The Council spent £1 on stamps.
3. Her sister lives in Scotland.
4. The Council will take her to Court.
5. The girl moved to Scotland last year.

B. Fill in the right word

1. She moved to the U.S.A. _____ year.
   (lost / list / last)
2. They sent her a final _____ Tax demand.
   (Pill / Poll / Pull)
3. She owes _____ 28 pence.
   (them / then / they)
4. Her sister _____ the Council.
   (ring / rung / rang)
5. They said they would _____ it off.
   (right / wrote / write)

C. Sort out these jumbled words

dias	ludow
hewn	yeth
madden	donces

D. Fill in the missing letters

1. Her si _ _ er rang the Council.
2. She had 7 d _ _ _ to pay.
3. A Scot _ _ _ _ girl moved to the U.S.A.
4. The Council sent her a second l _ tt _ r.
5. The P _ _ l Tax demand was for 28p.

E. Sort out these jumbled sentences

1. owes pence She 28 them.
2. to days She pay 7 had.
3. Council Her rang sister the.
4. court They would to her take.
5. two Council letters The sent.

F. Answer these questions

1. Where does the Scottish girl live now ?
2. Where did she live before ?
3. How much did she owe the Council ?
4. How many letters did the Council send ?
5. How much did each letter cost ?
6. What does *'write it off'* mean ?

Note: The Poll Tax was brought in to replace the old Rates system. It was introduced in Scotland a year before the rest of the U.K. It was very unpopular and was soon replaced by the Council Tax.

Brown and Brown / Basic Comprehension

'Street' to the top

After 30 years, *Coronation Street* is still the most popular programme on TV. Newer programmes, like *Neighbours* and *EastEnders*, have been top of the ratings for a time and, some years ago, the number of people watching *Coronation Street* dropped quite a lot. Now, numbers have picked up again and over 16 million people watch it each week. Not even the World Cup in June and July could beat the ever-popular 'Street'.

Autumn 1990

A. True / False / Maybe

1. *Coronation Street* started 30 years ago.
2. *Neighbours* is top of the ratings.
3. 16 million people watch *EastEnders*.
4. The World Cup was in June and July.
5. The World Cup had more viewers than *Coronation Street*.

B. Fill in the right word

1. *Coronation Street* is the _____ popular programme on TV.   *(must / most / mast)*
2. The number of people watching _____ quite a lot.   *(drooped / dripped / dropped)*
3. Numbers have _____ up again.   *(picked / packed / pecked)*
4. 16 million people _____ it each week.   *(witch / wash / watch)*

C. Fill in the missing word

1. Numbers have picked again.
2. *Coronation Street* is still the most programme on TV.
3. 16 million people it each week.
4. Newer programmes have been top of the ratings for time.

D. Which word is the odd one out ?

1. street   beat   been   week
2. popular   people   quite   picked
3. never   popular   number   ever
4. now   on   ago   not

E. TV Soap Operas

Make a list of the Soap Operas on TV at the moment. Which are the top 3 in the ratings ?

Food labels

From January 1st 1991 there is a new law about the labels on food. It is now illegal to sell food with a label which says *Sell by....* . Most chilled foods, like soft cheese, yoghurt and cooked meat, must have a label which says *Use by....* . It will be illegal to sell food after the *Use by....* date.

Many other foods, like bread, cakes, and biscuits, will have a label which says *Best before....* . These foods can still be sold after their *Best before....* date, but should be marked down in price and may be stale.

Spring 1991

A. True / False / Don't know
1. Yoghurt must now have a *Use by....* label.
2. Bread must now have a *Use by....* label.
3. Cakes must have a *Best before....* label.
4. Cooked meat must have a *Best before....* label.
5. Food should not be eaten after the *Use by....* date.

B. Fill in the missing word
1. From January 1st 1991 there is a new about food labels.
2. Soft cheese must have a *Use by....* .
3. Many other foods will a *Best before....* label.
4. It is illegal to food with a *Sell by....* label.
5. These foods should marked down in price.

C. Which word is the odd one out ?
1. biscuits   cheese   labels   meat
2. after   sold   before   now
3. legal   illegal   law   marked
4. says   these   their   the

D. Sort out the jumbled words

ewn	odof
tums	wond
bella	troughy
daber	repic

E. Yes / No / Maybe
1. Is it now illegal to sell food marked *Sell by....* ?
2. Is it now illegal to sell food marked *Best before....* ?
3. Is it legal to sell food marked *Use by....* ?
4. Is it legal to sell food after the *Best before....* date ?
5. Will you be ill if you eat food after the *Use by....* date ?

Riots

10 years after the last riots in inner cities, riots have happened again. This time they were in Oxford, Cardiff, Bristol and Newcastle. Most of the riots have been in run-down areas of the cities and, often, stolen cars have been driven at high speed around the areas by young kids. Local shops and buildings have been damaged or burnt down, but police have made few arrests.

Some people say that the riots were caused by unemployment, poor schools, bad housing, and cut-backs in money from Government. Others say that the riots were organised by a few people making trouble and getting others to join in.

Autumn 1991

A. True / False / Maybe

1. 10 years ago there were riots in Bristol.
2. All the riots were in run-down areas.
3. Stolen cars were driven by police.
4. Riots were caused by unemployment.
5. A few people organised the riots.
6. All local shops were burnt down.

B. Fill in the missing word

1. Police have made few.
2. Some people that the riots were caused by unemployment.
3. The Government has cut back to inner cities.
4. Stolen cars have been at high speed.
5. The last riots were 10 ago.

C. Fill in the missing vowels

(All the words can be found in the article)

yrs	hppnd	yng
hsng	schls	gttng
stln	rts	bldngs
nmplymnt	trbl	ppl

D. Opposites

Find a word in the article which means the opposite of each of these words:

old	adults	mended
good	many	before

E. What do you think ?

Finish the sentences below:

1. Riots happen ....
2. Young kids have ....
3. The Police should ....
4. The Government is ....
5. Cities have ....
6. Local people can ....
7. Parents need ....
8. Schools are ....

F. Word puzzle

Underline the words in the list below which can be made from the letters in:

unemployment

top	mean	lot	tent
yes	out	play	meet
pound	note	ten	let

Left up in the air

A 23-year-old man, Alan Anderson, was the passenger in a 2-seater plane when the pilot collapsed from a heart attack. The plane went out of control, but Mr. Anderson managed to drag the pilot to one side. He had never flown a plane before, but he worked out how to radio for help.

The pilot of another plane nearby, who was a flying instructor, went to his aid and gave him advice over the radio. They did some practice and then Mr. Anderson landed the plane safely at Cardiff airport.

Summer 1992

A. Answer these questions

1. What was the name of the passenger ?
2. What happened to the pilot ?
3. What happened to the plane ?
4. Who helped the passenger ?
5. At which airport did the plane land ?

B. True / False / Don't know

1. Mr. Anderson had never flown in a plane before.
2. Mr. Anderson had never flown a plane before.
3. Mr. Anderson had a heart attack.
4. The pilot was 23 years old.
5. The pilot dragged Mr. Anderson to one side.

C. Sort out the jumbled sentences

1. collapsed heart The attack a pilot from.
2. pilot him gave Another advice.
3. never He a before had plane flown.
4. managed pilot to He the to one drag side.
5. control The out of went plane.

D. Fill in the right word

1. The plane _____ out of control.
   (want / went / wont)
2. The plane landed _____ at Cardiff.
   (safety / safer / safely)
3. The flying _____ went to his aid.
   (instructor / instructed / instructing)
4. He _____ out how to radio for help.
   (worker / works / worked)
5. They _____ some practice.
   (dib / bid / did)

E. Looking carefully

1. How many numbers are there in the article ?
2. How many pilots are there in the article ?
3. Which words in the article contain double letters *(e.g. ss)* ?
4. Which words in the article contain the letter pattern *an* ?

Gold for Linford !

The men's 100 metres sprint is one of the highlights of the Olympic Games athletics events. Before the Games, most people thought that the Americans would win the gold medal for the third time in a row. But the British men's team captain, Linford Christie, had set his sights high after winning a silver medal in the 1988 Olympic Games.

In the Olympic final in Barcelona, he came storming through to win Britain's only gold medal in the men's athletics events. His years of hard training had paid off and, at the age of 32 years and 3 months, he became the oldest man ever to win an Olympic 100 metres title.

Autumn 1992

A. Yes / No / Maybe

1. Were the 1988 Olympic Games held in Barcelona ?
2. Is Christie the fastest runner in the world ?
3. Had Linford won an Olympic medal before?
4. Was Christie older than all the others in the final ?
5. Did the Americans win the last 3 Olympic 100 metres ?

B. Join up these half sentences

The British men's team captain.......

The 100 metres is one of the.......

In the Olympic final he came.......

He became the oldest man.......

Linford Christie.......

.......storming through to win.

.......had won a silver medal in 1988.

.......to win an Olympic 100 metres title.

.......had set his sights high.

.......highlights of the Olympic Games.

C. Fill in the missing word

1. Most people that the Americans would win.
2. Christie had set his high.
3. He won Britain's only medal.
4. His years hard training had paid off.
5. He won a medal in the1988 Olympic Games.

D. How many ?

How many words in the article

a. *Contain the spelling **th** ?*

b. *Contain the spelling **gh** ?*

c. *End in **s** ?*

E. Word game

Make a list of words containing 3 or more letters, using the letters in

athletics

Changing gear ?

In a recent case at Leicester Crown Court, the defendant was being cross-examined about reckless driving.

"So you then turned into Charles Street," said the barrister. "How fast were you going ?"

"Not more than 20 miles per hour," replied the defendant.

"And what gear were you in ?"

"Jeans and a T-shirt."

Spring 1993

A. Yes / No / Maybe

1. The case was at Leicester Crown Court.
2. Charles Street is in Leicester.
3. The barrister wore jeans.
4. The case was about reckless driving.
5. The defendant was female.

B. Fill in the missing word

1. "So then turned into Charles Street."
2. "How were you going ?"
3. "Not more than 20 per hour."
4. The defendant being cross-examined.
5. "And gear were you in ?"

C. Fill in the right word

1. The _____ was at Leicester Crown Court.
   (care / case / cane)
2. The driver was going _____ fast.
   (to / two / too)
3. The defendant _____ jeans.
   (were / wear / wore)
4. The speed was not _____ than 20 m.p.h.
   (moor / morn / more)
5. T-_____ are fashionable.
   (skirts / shirts / shorts)

D. Which word is the odd one out ?

1. being   driving   were   going
2. Leicester   miles   Court   Charles
3. examined   replied   said   turned
4. than   then   they   thin
5. how   what   more   when

E. Same meaning
Find a word in the article which means much the same as each of these:

careless   quick   answered

clothes   lawyer   trousers

F. Same spelling - different meaning
Put each of these words into a sentence which gives it a different meaning from the one in the article:

gear   court   fast   cross

G. Words within words
How many words can you find hidden in the words below ?
e.g. **crown** *has* **row** *and* **own** *hidden in it*

c h a n g i n g

d e f e n d a n t

c r o s s - e x a m i n e d

On top of the world

40 years ago, on June 1st 1953, the *Times* newspaper in London had a 'scoop'. Their reporter in Nepal had sent a message in code. The decoded message was printed in the paper's first edition the next day. It said: "Summit of Everest reached on May 29th by Hillary and Tenzing". The timing was perfect. The news of the British team's success came on the morning of the coronation of Queen Elizabeth II. Britain was on top of the world !

Summer 1993

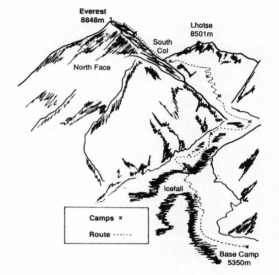

A. True / False / Maybe

1. The summit of Everest was reached on June 1st.
2. The coronation was on June 2nd.
3. The *Sunday Times* had a 'scoop'.
4. The message was in code.
5. Everest is the world's highest mountain.

B. Answer these questions

1. Why do you think the message was sent in code ?
2. What is a 'scoop' ?
3. In which group of mountains is Everest ?
   a. the Andes   b. the Himalayas   c. the Rockies
4. How high is Everest ?
   a. about 7,000m   b. about 8,000m   c. about 9,000m

C. Sort out these jumbled sentences

1. was forty Queen ago The crowned years.
2. summit Tenzing the reached and Everest of Hillary.
3. day message the printed next was The.
4. the world top of Britain was on.

> ### Did you know?
>
> Sir John Hunt, leader of the 1953 Everest Expedition, failed his R.A.F. medical before the war.
>
> They told him to be careful when climbing stairs!

D. Word meanings

1. *Give a word or phrase which means the same as each of these:*
   summit   **message**   **next**   **reached**

2. *Give a word which means the opposite of each of these:*
   success   **perfect**   **first**   **morning**

Balloon crash cuts off power

A hot-air balloon crashed into an 11,000 volt cable on Saturday night. It cut off electricity to 300 homes near Tenbury Wells. Luckily, none of the nine passengers was hurt when the balloon came down on Oldwood Common. The pilot said it was misty and he didn't see the cable until he was three yards from it. Olive York, who lives close by, said she saw a blue flash as the balloon hit the cable. The basket was black down one side where it had been scorched.

Autumn 1993

A. True / False / Maybe

1. The pilot was a man.
2. Tenbury Wells had no electricity on Saturday night.
3. Olive York was in the balloon.
4. The pilot was to blame for the crash.
5. The crash happened in daylight.

B. Fill in the right word

1. The balloon cut off electricity _____ 300 homes.
   (to / too / two)

2. Olive York _____ a blue flash.
   (sore / saw / was)

3. The basket was black down _____ side.
   (won / on / one)

4. The pilot did not see the cable until he was three yards _____ it.
   (form / from / for)

5. The balloon crashed into an _____ cable.
   (electric / electricity / electrical)

C. Finish these sentences in your own words

1. Hot air balloons are......
2. Flying in a balloon would......
3. A volt is......
4. It was lucky that......
5. 'A *lot of hot air*' means.......

Business lunch

A businessman in Brighton, Mr. Reddall, has banked with Barclays for 20 years. Each year he has a meeting with the bank manager to discuss his bank account. In the last few years he has taken the manager out for lunch.

This December, he took the new manager out for lunch and paid the £40 bill. A few weeks later, he got his bank statement from Barclays. He had been charged £110 for 2 hours and 5 minutes of the bank manager's time !

Spring 1994

A. Yes / No / Don't know

1. Does Mr. Reddall have a business in Brighton ?
2. Has Mr. Reddall banked with Barclays for 10 years ?
3. Did the bank manager pay for the lunch ?
4. Did the lunch last for 2 hours and 5 minutes ?
5. Did Mr. Reddall pay the £110 bank charge ?

B. Fill in the missing word

1. Mr. Reddall has banked with Barclays ___ 20 years.
2. Each year ___ has a meeting with the bank manager.
3. In the ___ few years he has taken the manager out for lunch.
4. This December he took the new ___ out for lunch.
5. He had been ___ £110 for the manager's time.

C. Join up these half sentences

A charge of £110	by Mr. Reddall.
A businessman in Brighton	over lunch.
The lunch was paid for	banked with Barclays.
He got his statement	had been made for the manager's time.
They discussed his account	a few weeks later.

D. Answer these questions

1. How much time did the bank manager charge for, in minutes ?
2. Use a calculator to work out how much the manager charged per minute of his time.
3. Use a calculator to work out how much the manager charged per hour of his time.
4. Business people often say, "There's no such thing as a free lunch." What do they mean ?

The Isles of Dogs

Britain is said to be a nation of dog lovers. One household in four has a dog and quite a number of them have more than one. On average, dog owners spend £750 a year on their pets and, as a nation, we spend over a billion pounds a year feeding them. One dog in two sleeps in its owner's bedroom and one dog in five goes to a dog hairdressing salon each month !

But a lot of people don't like dogs and each year about 100 children and adults lose the sight in an eye because of disease from dog droppings.

Summer 1994

A. True / False / Maybe

1. 1 household in 4 has a dog.
2. 1 dog in 5 sleeps in the house.
3. People in the British Isles love dogs.
4. Most dogs cost over £10 a week.
5. 1 in 2 owners sleeps in the doghouse.

B. Fill in the missing word

1. Britain is said to be a nation of lovers.
2. On average, dog owners £750 a year on their pets.
3. 1 dog in 5 goes a dog hairdressing salon each month.
4. A lot of people don't dogs.
5. About 100 children and adults lose the sight an eye.

C. Sort out these jumbled words

   gods   tuqie   intano   nerow   leepop

D. Change the vowel

The five vowels are: **a   e   i   o   u**
You can change the vowel in the word **than** *to make the words* **th<u>e</u>n** *and* **th<u>i</u>n**.

How many words can you make by changing the vowel in each of these words ?

   dog   **on**   **but**   **as**   **lot**   **pet**

E. Phrases

There are a lot of well-known phrases with the word **dog** *in them.*
   e.g. every dog has his day; dog-tired

How many other phrases can you think of with **dog** *in them ?*

A flash in the pan

A woman threw a cockroach into the toilet. When it wouldn't drown, she sprayed it with a lot of fly spray. Later, her husband went to the toilet and dropped a lighted cigarette into the W.C. pan. The fly spray was set on fire by the cigarette and the husband got some very painful burns. The ambulance men who came to take him to hospital laughed so much that they dropped the stretcher on the way down the stairs. The husband ended up in hospital with a broken pelvis and ribs !

Autumn 1994

A. Yes / No / Maybe

1. Did the woman find the cockroach ?
2. Could the cockroach swim ?
3. Did the fly spray kill the cockroach ?
4. Did the husband smoke ?
5. Did the cigarette start the fire ?
6. Was the woman hurt in the fire ?
7. Did the husband and wife live in a flat ?
8. Did the ambulance men drop the stretcher at the top of the stairs ?
9. Did the wife laugh at her husband ?
10. Did the husband break his leg ?

B. Sort out these jumbled words

ryve   manow   lottie   tegicerat   shalipot

C. Answer these questions

1. *Who was most to blame for the accident ?*
   a. The woman   b. The husband   c. The ambulance men

2. *What is the moral of the story ?*
   a. Don't smoke   b. Don't use fly spray   c. Don't laugh

D. Spelling

1. *Find a word in the story which contains the same double vowel sound as each of these:*
   r**oa**d   b**oi**l   r**ai**n

2. *Find words in the story which begin with the same letters as each of these:*
   string   **dr**ag   **wh**ere   **spr**ead   **th**is   **br**ick

The end of the line ?

At the end of 1994, an opinion poll showed that only 1 in 3 people thought we would still have a Royal Family in 50 years' time. Most people expected that Britain would become a Republic, and they said that they would prefer to have a President who was not political.

Hardly a month goes by now without the newspapers printing 'shocking' headlines about the Royal family. But why is there so much fuss ? Henry VIII had six wives. Charles II's famous mistress was Nell Gwynn, an actress. Today, at least half of all marriages have problems, so why should we expect the Royal Family to be any better than others in public life ?

Spring 1995

The last queen ?

A. Yes / No / Maybe
1. 1 in 3 is about 30%.
2. 50 years is half a century.
3. Britain will become a Republic.
4. The President would be a politician.
5. Every day there is shocking news about the Royal family.
6. Henry VII had six wives.
7. Prince Charles would become King Charles III.
8. Prince Charles could become President.

B. Which is the odd one out ?
1. Charles   Nell   Henry   Gwynn
2. actress   princess   mistress   fuss   success
3. VIII   3   1   50   94
4. what   why   would   who   when
5. headlines   people   newspapers   President   wives

C. Sort out these jumbled words
ubato   flah   refrep   yotad   loary

D. Words within words
How many words can you think of which contain the word **end** *?*
e.g. spend*ing*

E. Choose a President
Write a sentence saying who you would choose as President of Britain, and why.

On the wrong track

British Rail have done it again. First, trains were being delayed because there were leaves on the track. Then trains were delayed because of the wrong sort of snow. Now a train has been delayed because the driver didn't know the way!

Last month, the 19.10 from Cardiff to Birmingham stopped 7 miles out of Birmingham. The conductor announced to the 100 passengers, "We apologise for the delay - the driver doesn't know the way."

The train had been diverted because of track repairs. Train drivers have to be trained for each route they drive and this driver didn't know the diversion route. A replacement driver was sent and the train arrived at Birmingham New Street 40 minutes late.

Summer 1995

A. Yes / No / Maybe

1. Trains have been delayed for three different reasons.
2. The 7.10 p.m. from Cardiff was delayed.
3. There were 1000 passengers on the train.
4. The train was diverted because of snow.
5. The driver hadn't been trained.
6. The train was over half an hour late.

Excuse me. Is this the way to Birmingham?

B. Same spelling - different meaning

Put each of these words into a sentence which gives it a different meaning from the one in the article.

train	leaves	track	drive	late

C. Word meanings

Find a word in the article which means much the same as each of these:

sent another way   not right   a way from one place to another

be sorry   substitute   reported   held back

D. Word game

Make a list of words containing 2 or more letters, using letters from :

1. **BRITISH RAIL**   2. **BIRMINGHAM**

Another near miss

Nuclear Electric has recently been fined £250,000 at Mold Crown Court because of an accident 2 years ago. Health and Safety Inspectors claimed in Court that the company had put profits before safety and could have caused a very serious accident. The accident at Wylfa Power Station on Anglesey happened when part of a crane dropped into one of the reactor's gas tubes. Staff took 9 hours to shut down the reactor.

Nuclear Electric denied that there had been any danger but they agreed that staff had not made the right decisions. The incident highlights, once again, public concern over nuclear power and plans to privatise it.

Autumn 1995

A. Yes / No / Maybe

1. Nuclear Electric was fined a quarter of a million pounds.
2. The accident happened over a year ago.
3. The company had put profits before safety.
4. A crane fell into a reactor tube.
5. It took 6 hours to shut down the reactor.
6. There was no danger to the public.
7. Nuclear Electric apologised to the court.
8. People are worried about nuclear power.

*Mark **Anglesey** & **Mold** on the map*

B. How many ?

Answer these questions by looking quickly through the news item.

1. How many words have capital letters ?
2. How many numbers are there in the news item ?
3. How many sentences are there ?
4. How many paragraphs are there ?
5. How many words begin with *c* as in *can* ?

C. Word meanings

1. *Find a word in the news item which means the same as each of these:*

    lately   **occurred**   **workers**   **anxiety**

2. *Find a word in the news item which means the opposite of each of these:*

    danger   **losses**   **open**   **wrong**

D. What do you think ?

What do you think about nuclear power ? Write down your views in a few sentences.

Frank walks in on his wake

A group of businessmen in Carlisle got the fright of their lives recently. They were meeting at their club to mourn the death of one of their group, Frank Ellwood, from the village of Scotby, when Frank walked in. He was greeted by shocked faces all round.

The thing was that Frank Ellwood of Scotby *had* died but, unknown to everyone, there were two Frank Ellwoods in the village. The surviving Frank, a former bank manager, found out that friends had been telephoning each other with the news of his death. Some of them had even arranged to go to the funeral of the wrong Frank. One friend met him in the street and she thought she had seen a ghost !

Frank joked about it all afterwards. He said that his friends had all rung each other to say he had died, but nobody had told him !

Spring 1996

A. True / False / Maybe

1. Frank Ellwood had died.
2. Frank Ellwood had been a bank manager.
3. Scotby is a village near Carlisle.
4. The bank manager's funeral was in Scotby.
5. Frank Ellwood was a member of the club.
6. Frank didn't think what had happened was funny.

B. Word meanings

Give a word or phrase which means the same as each of these words from the article:

mourn   **shocked**   **surviving**   **greeted**   **recently**   **arranged**

C. Spelling

Give one other word which contains the same spelling pattern as each of these words from the article:

wrong (**wr**)   fright (**ght**)   unknown (**kn**)   walked (**lk**)

What do all these spelling patterns have in common ?

D. Writing

1. *Explain in a few sentences how you think the mistake happened.*
2. *Choose one of the 2 Frank Ellwoods and write a few sentences describing him.*

Homeless

I've been sleeping rough for about 9 months.

Most nights I sleep out but sometimes I go to a hostel.

I left home when I was 16.

I couldn't stand it any longer.

My old man was always getting at me.

I had a bad time for a year or so.

I grew up fast - learned the hard way.

Then I met Lisa.

We were together for 3 or 4 years.

I got a regular job and we had a flat.

A couple of years ago, things started to go wrong.

We had to get out of the flat.

We joined a squat but then my job finished.

Lisa left.

I went on the booze - just like my dad.

I'm off it now, more or less.

What I really need is somewhere to live.

Summer 1996

A. True / False / Maybe

1. He usually sleeps in a hostel.
2. His old man made him leave home.
3. He has never had a job.
4. He is aged 24.
5. He went on the booze because Lisa left him.
6. His Dad was a drunk.

B. What do you think ?

1. It is his fault that he has ended up sleeping rough.
2. If he had had good housing, everything would have been all right.
3. His problems were caused by his parents.
4. Lisa should have stuck by him.
5. Better hostels are the answer for the homeless.
6. It is even more important to combat homelessness than unemployment.

Smoke detector saves life

A man got fed up with his smoke detector going off each time he had a fry-up. So he took out the battery and taped it to the ceiling.

A few days later, he decided to have some chips and put the chip pan on to heat up. Then he sat down in a chair and fell fast asleep. The pan soon caught fire but the smoke and the burning fat didn't wake him. The heat in the kitchen began to rise and the tape started to peel off the ceiling.

The man finally woke up when the battery hit him on the head !

Autumn 1996

A. Yes / No / Maybe

1. The man taped his smoke detector to the ceiling.
2. A week later he had some chips.
3. He fell asleep and the pan caught fire.
4. The chips were burnt.
5. The battery fell in the chip pan.
6. The kitchen needed re-decorating.
7. The man was unharmed.
8. The smoke detector saved his life.

B. Which word is the odd one out ?

1. fell   fed   fat   off   few
2. pan   man   got   fast   sat
3. heat   each   peel   head   asleep
4. time   fire   smoke   fry   wake
5. fell   battery   off   chips   finally

C. Finish these phrases

1. There's no smoke.....
2. If you can't stand the heat.....
3. Out of the frying pan.....
4. He's had his.....
5. Don't play with.....

D. *Up* and *Off*

1. The man in the article had a ***fry-up***.
   *How many words can you think of which contain -**up** ?*
   e.g. send-up   warm-up

2. *How many words can you think of which contain -**off** ?*
   e.g. take-off   show-off

Polishing them off

Doctors in South Africa have at last managed to solve the mystery of a series of hospital deaths. Several patients in a hospital in Orange Free State died on Friday mornings. Each patient had been in the same bed in the same ward. The patients were all on a vital life-support machine.

The doctors have now discovered that on Friday mornings the same cleaner was on duty. She came in to polish the floors. She unplugged the machine and plugged in her floor polisher. When she had finished, she plugged the life-support machine back in and went on her way.

Spring 1997

A. Yes or No ?

1. Was the hospital in South Africa ?
2. Did all the patients use the same bed ?
3. Did the cleaner polish the floors by hand ?
4. Was the life-support machine electric ?
5. Was the cleaner a man ?

B. Fill in the right word

1. Patients _____ on Friday mornings.
   (dead / dyed / deed / died)
2. They had _____ in the same bed.
   (bean / been / ben / dean)
3. The patients _____ on a machine.
   (wore / wear / where / were)
4. The doctors have _____ discovered....
   (new / know / now / knew)
5. She _____ on her way.
   (when / want / won't / went)

C. True / False / Don't know

1. The doctors solved the mystery.
2. The patients died on Friday mornings.
3. The cleaner only worked on Fridays.
4. The life-support machine was on all the time.
5. The cleaner killed the patients.

D. Fill in the missing word

1. Patients died Friday mornings.
2. Each patient had been the same bed.
3. The patients were on a life-support.
4. She came in to the floors.
5. She went her way.

E. Which word is the odd one out ?

1. doctors   patients   hospital   cleaners
2. managed   came   died   discovered
3. all   support   of   plugged
4. her   were   ward   several
5. she   patients   machine   mystery

F. Sort out the jumbled words

evah	hasted
livat	gulpged
meas	slipho

G. Same meaning - different words

1. ***Polish off*** is one way of saying ***kill***
   *Write down other words or phrases which mean the same as **kill**.*
2. *Write down other words or phrases which mean the same as **died**.*

A deadly error

Western Australia must hold the record for the daftest election result.

In 1974, the mayor of a town in Western Australia died. A by-election was held to find a new mayor. The local town hall made an error on the ballot paper and kept the dead mayor's name on the list. He was re-elected by 8,731 votes for another year.

His sister-in-law said, "I know that George was very popular. But I was still very surprised to hear the result on the radio as I was driving back from the crematorium."

Summer 1997

A. Yes or No ?

1. Was the town in Western Austria ?
2. Was the old mayor very popular ?
3. Had the new mayor died ?
4. Was George re-elected ?
5. Was the election result on the radio ?

B. Fill in the missing word

1. A by-election held to find a new mayor.
2. The local hall made an error.
3. I know George was very.
4. I was still very to hear the result.
5. I was back from the crematorium.

C. True / False / Maybe

1. All mayors in Australia are elected.
2. The by-election was in 1974.
3. The town hall made a spelling error.
4. The old mayor was cremated.
5. George was married.

D. Same sound - different spelling

Find a word in the article which sounds like each of these but is spelt differently.

four	maid	no	here
dyed	fined	knew	haul

E. Sort out the jumbled words

drocer	preap
romay	blotal
stove	rustle

F. Beginnings and endings

1. *Find a word in the article which begins with the same 2 letters as each of these:*

   start   drink   knock   crisp

2. *Find a word in the article which ends with the same 2 letters as each of these:*

   down   final   word   best

3. *Find a word in the article which has the same first and last letters as each of these:*

   hand   spend   more   your

G. Opposites

Find a word in the article which means the opposite of each of these:

lose   off   alive   disliked

H. Word puzzle

Make a list of words with 2 or more letters using the letters in:

CREMATORIUM

Bats in the Attic

This summer, the Head Gardener on the Attingham Estate in Shropshire noticed that there was a nasty smell coming from the attic of his cottage. He found that the smell was being made by bats. Not just a few bats - there were 769 of them. They were getting in and out of the attic through a very small crack in the eaves.

The bats have turned out to be pipistrelles - the smallest of Britain's bats. This is thought to be one of the largest colonies in the U.K. Pipistrelles are protected by law, so a special entrance and exit has now been made for them.

It seems that the gardener will just have to put up with the smell !

Autumn 1997

A. True / False / Maybe

1. The Head Gardener lives in Shropshire.

2. There was a nasty smell in his attic.

3. Bats were getting in down the chimney.

4. The bats were very big.

5. The gardener cannot kill the bats.

6. The gardener will have to move.

B. Yes / No / Don't know

1. Do bats only fly at night ?

2. Are bats blind ?

3. Are bats mammals ?

4. Are all British bats protected by law ?

C. Word meanings

1. What is an *Estate* ?

2. What are the *eaves* of a house ?

3. What is a *colony* ?

4. *Think of a word which means the same as each of these words from the article:*
   nasty   **smell**   **small**   **noticed**   **getting**

5. *Think of a word which means the opposite of each of these words from the article:*
   coming   **few**   **in**   **smallest**   **now**

D. Word game

Make a list of words with 2 or more letters, using the letters in:

P I P I S T R E L L E

Drunk in charge

When officials arrived at Bradford's No. 1 Court, they were faced with a problem. The door leading from the court to the cells was jammed and no one could open it. The police tried and the Court caretaker tried but the lock would not turn.

In the end, Tom Ward, aged 45, a man on a 'drunk and disorderly' charge, came to the rescue. He kicked the door open and the business of the Court began.

Spring 1998

A. True / False / Maybe

1. The door to the cells was locked.
2. The caretaker kicked open the door.
3. Tom Ward was aged 54.
4. Tom Ward was stronger than the caretaker.
5. Tom Ward was drunk.

B. Fill in the right word

1. Officials arrived at Bradford's No. 1 _____ . *(Count / Caught / Court)*
2. The door _____ the cells was jammed. *(to / too / two)*
3. No _____ could open it. *(on / won / one)*
4. The _____ would not turn. *(lack / loch / lock / luck)*
5. Tom Ward _____ the door open. *(kick / kicked / killed)*

C. Fill in the missing word

1. They were faced with problem.
2. The to the cells was jammed.
3. The police tried and the Court tried.
4. Tom Ward came the rescue.
5. The business of the began.

D. Sort out these jumbled words

rodo	madjem
coplie	knurd
secure	bange

E. Words within words

How many words can you find hidden in each of these words, without changing the order of the letters ? List them under each word.

business　　　　　　　　**disorderly**　　　　　　　　**caretaker**

The village postman

An Italian village postman must claim the record for being the worst postman of all time.

He began work in 1995. On his first day, he ran over his postmistress in his van and then, accidentally, set fire to the sorting office. In 1996, he lost all the village's Christmas post after crashing his van into the river.

During the next 12 months, he had to be rescued on 7 different occasions after getting his hand stuck in letter boxes. The final straw came when he ran over his postmistress for a second time. After this, he was sacked.

His boss said, "We had to tell him by telephone because his letter of dismissal got lost in the post."

Summer 1998

A. Yes / No / Maybe

1. The postman was an Italian.
2. He was the postman for only one village.
3. He set fire to the sorting office on his first day.
4. His boss was a woman.
5. He ran over the postmistress on his last day.

B. Fill in the missing word

1. He began in 1995.
2. On his first day, he ran his postmistress in his van.
3. He had to rescued on 7 different occasions.
4. On 7 different occasions he got his hand stuck in boxes.
5. His letter of dismissal lost in the post.

C. Sort out these jumbled sentences

1. work 1995 began in he.
2. van the river he his into crashed.
3. post village's lost all he the Christmas.
4. was this sacked he after.
5. the postman time of he worst was all.

D. Words within words

How many words can you find hidden in these words ? (***e.g. or** is hidden in **worst***)

accidental   **crashing**   **postmistress**

It's in the bag !

A Glasgow man went to a car boot sale. He bought a bag of old penny pieces for £2.50. The sellers had found them when they were clearing out their great-aunt's house. Amongst the pennies was another coin which the sellers thought was just a cheap brass token.

The buyer took the 'token' to a coin dealer in Glasgow. The dealer, Richard Green, was amazed to see it. He said it was a James VI four-pound piece, worth about £6,000.

The owner of the coin, who has been out of work for fifteen years, will sell it. He said that he would take his family on holiday for the first time in years.

Autumn 1998

A. Yes / No / Maybe

1. The buyer was from Glasgow.
2. The buyer's name was Richard Green.
3. The bag of pennies cost £3.50.
4. The brass token was worth £4.
5. The buyer had been out of work for 15 years.
6. The buyer was married.

B. Which is the odd one out ?

1. seller   buyer   coin   dealer   owner
2. Glasgow   Richard   man   James   Green
3. bought   bag   brass   out   been
4. four   VI   thousand   fifteen   pennies

C. Fill in the missing word

1. A man went to a car boot sale.
2. He bought bag of old penny pieces.
3. The buyer the token to a coin dealer.
4. He said it was a VI four-pound piece.
5. The owner of the coin will it.

D. Sort out these jumbled words

cipees	doilhay
icon	relade
tuna	worne
boguth	throw

E. What do you think ?

1. How old was the brass token ?
2. Was the dealer an honest man ?
3. What sort of holiday might the family have ?

A night on the tiles ?

A Hammersmith man was involved in a fight in the Palais night club. Bouncers from the club chased the man across the rooftops. The man managed to escape from the bouncers with a daring leap on to a nearby roof. He then dropped through the skylight on the roof. He found himself in the custody room of Hammersmith police station. He was arrested and charged with assault.

Welcome to our new drop-in service....

A. True / False / Maybe

1. There was a fight at the Palais night club.
2. The Palais night club is in Hammersmith.
3. The Club bouncers started the fight.
4. The man was chased across the rooftops.
5. He leapt on to the roof of the police station.
6. He gave himself up to the police.

B. Find the mistake in each sentence

1. A Hammersmith man was involved in a night.
2. There was a fight in the Palais light club.
3. The man made a daring heap on to a nearby roof.
4. He found himself in the custard room of Hammersmith police station.
5. He was arrested and charged with a salt.

C. Join up these half words

sky	smith
Hammer	tops
roof	by
near	light

D. Same word - different meaning

Put each of these words into a sentence which gives it a different meaning from the one in the article above.

club   **station**   **leap**   **charged**   **bouncer**

Fed up

A man walked into a *Burger King* in Michigan, U.S.A. at 7.50 a.m. He pulled out a gun and demanded cash from a cashier. The cashier said that he could not open the tills unless he had a food order.

The man ordered onion rings. The cashier said that onion rings were not available for breakfast. The man got fed up and walked away.

But I always have onion rings for breakfast ......

A. Yes / No / Maybe

1. Did the man want some food ?
2. Did the man get some cash from the cashier ?
3. Did the man have a gun ?
4. Could the man have ordered onion rings at 7.50 p.m. ?
5. Did the cashier get fed up ?

B. Join up these half sentences

He demanded	pulled out a gun.
The man	into a *Burger King*.
A man walked	ordered onion rings.
He	up and walked away.
The man got fed	cash from a cashier.

C. Fill in the missing vowels
(*All the words are taken from the news item above*)

mn	**gn**	**rngs**	**fd**	**tlls**
tht	**csh**	**th**	**Kng**	**wlkd**

D. Fill in the missing consonants
(*All the words are taken from the news item above*)

pu _ _ ed	**ca _ _**	**cou _ _**	**unle _ _**
ti _ _ s	**ri _ _ s**	**availa _ _ e**	**_ _ eakfast**

E. How many ?

1. *How many words in the news item end in* ***ed*** *?*
2. *How many words in the news item contain the letters* ***er*** *?*

The wrong end of the stick

During World War II, the Army asked its top brass to improve the design of the hand grenade. Army staff had reported that the metal grenades often bounced off tanks and guns. They asked if grenades could be made softer, so that they didn't bounce.

One designer took this idea a step further. He invented the sticky grenade (*Code name - the 74(ST)*) which would stick to enemy tanks. During training, they found that it had one drawback. The person throwing it couldn't let go of it ! The sticky grenade didn't catch on.

A. True / False / Maybe

1. Grenades were used in World War II.
2. All grenades were made of metal.
3. The army wanted tanks to be made softer.
4. The **74(ST)** was designed by one man.
5. The **74(ST)** would stick to tanks.

B. Fill in the right word

1. The army wanted to improve the design of the _____ grenade.
   (*hard / hand / hound*)
2. Metal grenades often bounced off _____ and guns.
   (*tanks / thanks / talks*)
3. They _____ if grenades could be made softer.
   (*ask / asks / asked*)
4. They found that it had _____ drawback.
   (*on / won / one*)
5. _____ sticky grenade didn't catch on.
   (*they / thee / the*)

C. How many ?

1. How many times is the word *grenade* used in the article ?
2. How many times is the word *of* used in the article ?
3. How many times is the word *the* used in the article ?
4. How many words contain the spelling pattern *ou* ?
5. How many words contain the spelling pattern *ing* ?

*Brown and Brown / **Basic Comprehension***

Stepping out

Many years ago, a man from West London went to take his driving test for a motor scooter. He was told to drive round a certain route and that he would be watched by a hidden examiner. At some point, the examiner would step out in front of him to test his braking skill.

The man drove round the route but no examiner appeared. He drove round again, but still no examiner stepped out in front of him. He went back to the Test Centre and asked what had happened.

"Sorry !" he was told. "The examiner stepped in front of the wrong scooter !"

A. Yes / No / Maybe

1. Did the driving test take place in West London ?
2. Was the driving test for a motorbike ?
3. Did the man drive round the test route twice ?
4. Did the examiner step out in front of him ?
5. Did the man pass his driving test ?

B. Fill in the missing word

1. A man went to take his driving test for a motor.
2. He was told to drive round certain route.
3. The man drove round the route no examiner appeared.
4. He went back to the Centre.
5. The examiner in front of the wrong scooter.

C. Join up these half words
(The whole words are in the article above)

driv	er
cer	ry
hid	ing
sor	den
scoot	tain

D. Words within words
How many words can you find within the words below ?
*e.g. The word **motor** contains **to**, **tor** and **or***

watched	examiner	braking	appeared

A spare part

Mr. Watson's vacuum cleaner broke down one day. He worked out that only a very small part in the speed control unit needed replacing. He rang *Miele*, the company who made it, and was told they could only supply the whole unit, which would cost £72.50 including postage. This seemed far too expensive.

He then rang a high-street electrical shop. They said that they had the part and it would cost him only 89p. Later that day, Mr. Watson enquired at his local repair shop, which was doing some other work for him. He was given the part free of charge. It pays to shop around !

A. True / False / Maybe

1. The vacuum cleaner was made by *Miele*.
2. The speed control unit needed replacing.
3. The speed control unit cost £72.50, not including postage.
4. Mr. Watson went into his local repair shop later that day.
5. He got the part for only 89p.

B. Join up these half sentences

He was given the part	only 89p.
It pays to	broke down one day.
It would cost him	far too expensive
Mr. Watson's vacuum cleaner	shop around.
This seemed	free of charge.

C. Fill in a different word

Fill in each gap with a word which is different from the one used in the article.

1. Only a very _____ part in the speed control unit needed replacing.
2. He was told they could only supply the _____ unit.
3. This seemed far too _____ .
4. He then _____ a high-street electrical shop.
5. Mr. Watson _____ at his local repair shop.

D. Spelling

1. Write down all the words in the article which contain the spelling *ar*.
2. Write down all the words in the article which contain the spelling *ee*.

Brown and Brown / Basic Comprehension

The gentle gorilla

Some years ago, at Jersey Zoo, a father lifted his five-year old son on to a wall to see the gorillas. The boy fell 12 feet into the pit below and split his head open. The gorillas all moved towards the boy. But the largest gorilla, Jambo, sent the others away. He sat by the boy, stroked his back and protected him.

Two keepers tried to move the gorillas back into their shelter. All of them went - except one young male. A brave ambulance man jumped down into the pit. He had to check the boy over before he could be moved. The young gorilla ran around angrily and threw stones at them all. In the end, everyone did get out safely. The boy was badly hurt but he has recovered.

Jambo, the gentle giant, died at the early age of 31. There is now a life-size statue of him at the zoo.

A. Yes / No / Maybe

1. The zoo is in the Channel Isles.
2. The gorillas split the boy's head open.
3. Jambo was the largest gorilla.
4. Jambo stroked the boy's arm.
5. There were two keepers on duty.
6. The young gorilla threw stones.
7. The ambulance man was hurt.
8. Jambo died at age 13.

Jambo at Jersey Zoo
(above and below left)

B. Fill in the missing word

1. The boy ___ 12 feet into the pit below.
2. The gorillas all moved ___ the boy.
3. A ___ ambulance man jumped down into the pit.
4. The boy was badly ___ but he has recovered.
5. Jambo, the ___ giant, died at the early age of 31.

C. Sort out the jumbled words

wobel	pilst
therles	vaber
grainyl	ruth
legnet	tautse

D. Endings and beginnings

1. *Make a list of all the words in the article which end in* **y**.
2. *Make a list of all the words in the article which end in* **ed**.
3. *Make a list of all the words in the article which begin with* **b**.

A fair cuppa

When we buy most brands of tea and coffee, we are not paying a fair price to the people who grow it. Tea and coffee are grown in Third World countries. They are often a country's main export. The big tea and coffee companies force farmers to accept lower prices. For example, if a farmer has a bad harvest because of the weather, he should be able to charge more for his produce. But a big company can simply go and buy its tea or coffee elsewhere.

We often pay less than 1p for the tea in our cup. If we pay a little more - say, an extra 0.3p per cup - we can buy tea for which the farmer has been paid a fair price. Fairly traded tea and coffee are on sale in supermarkets, in charity shops such as Oxfam, and by mail order. The coffee is called *Cafédirect* and the tea is called *Teadirect*.

A. Answer these questions

1. Which countries grow tea and coffee ?
2. Do we pay the grower a fair price for tea and coffee ?
3. Do big companies pay growers a fair price for tea and coffee ?
4. What is the rough price of a cup of tea ?
5. What is meant by 'fair trading' ?
6. Where are fairly traded tea and coffee sold ?

B. Opposites
Find a word in the article which means the opposite of each of these words:

higher   import   less   sell   small   rarely   good

C. Same sound - different spelling
Find a word in the article which sounds the same as each of these but has a different spelling and meaning:

by   fare   groan   mane   witch   bean   male

D. Finish these sentences in your own words

1. We do not pay......
2. The big companies......
3. Farmers in the Third World should get......
4. *Cafédirect* is......
5. *Cuppa* is slang for......

Accidents can happen

Every day, someone has to climb one of England's highest mountains to report on the weather. A man and a woman do the job. One of them goes up Helvellyn every day for a week. The next week, the other one goes up each day. They record wind speed and temperature and fell-top conditions for the Lake District's winter Weatherline.

In February 1999, the man slipped and fell 200 feet. He broke his pelvis and hip and injured his side with his ice axe. He was airlifted off the mountain and ended up in hospital in Manchester for an operation. His partner said he was a very experienced and well-equipped climber. It just shows that accidents can happen to anyone.

Helvellyn - Striding Edge

A. Yes / No / Maybe

1. Does a weather watcher climb Helvellyn every day ?
2. Is Helvellyn England's highest mountain ?
3. Did the weather man fall 200 feet ?
4. Was he airlifted to hospital in Manchester ?
5. Was it his fault that he fell ?

B. Which word is the odd one out ?

1. hip   side   man   pelvis
2. wind   weather   temperature   winter
3. slipped   ended   broke   injured
4. England   Manchester   Weatherline   Helvellyn

C. Word meanings

Think of a word or phrase which means the same as each of these words from the article:

goes up   record   slipped   injured   fell-top

D. How many ?

1. How many sentences are there in the article ?
2. How many capital letters are there in the article ?
3. How many words in the article end with ***ed*** ?
4. How many times does the word ***and*** appear in the article ?
5. How many words can you make from the letters in each of these words from the article ?

   a. Weatherline   b. temperature   c. experienced

A shy best-seller

A list of the best-selling authors of the last ten years has been published. No one will be surprised by the name at the top of the list. It is Catherine Cookson, the writer from the North-East of England, who died in 1998. Her romantic, gritty stories appeal to millions. Many of her books have been made into TV dramas.

But few people would guess the name of the author who comes second. He is Dr. David Hessayon and he writes gardening books. His cheap, basic books, such as *The House Plant Expert* and *Be Your Own Garden Expert*, have sold well for the last 40 years. In that time, he has sold 40 million books. He never appears in public or on TV. But his books are always on the shelves of most garden centres, DIY superstores and bookshops.

A.   Answer these questions

1.   What sort of list is it ?

2.   What period of time does it cover ?

3.   Who is top of the list ?

4.   Where is she from ?

5.   What sort of books did she write ?

6.   When did she die ?

7.   Who is second on the list ?

8.   What sort of books does he write ?

9.   How long have his books been in the shops ?

10. Where can you buy his books ?

B.   Fill in the missing word

1.   Her romantic, gritty _____ appeal to millions.

2.   Many of her _____ have been made into TV dramas.

3.   He is Dr. David Hessayon and he _____ gardening books.

4.   In that time, he has sold 40 _____ books.

5.   He _____ appears in public or on TV.

C.   Fit together the half words

Fit together these half words to make five words from the article:

| sur- | -stores | roman- | -dening | pub- |
| -tic | gar- | -lished | super- | -prised |

The whole hog

The phrase *the whole hog* means *the lot* or *everything*. It came into use a few hundred years ago. The shilling coin used to have the king's head on one side. On the other side was a picture of a pig. So the coin became known as a 'hog'.

The coin was scored deeply across the middle with 2 lines. This was so that it could be broken in half or into quarters. Someone could then spend just a quarter or half a hog. Or they could be rash and spend the lot - the whole hog.

A. True / False / Maybe

1. *The whole hog* means *the lot*.
2. The phrase has been used for a hundred years.
3. The shilling coin had a pig's head on it.
4. The coin was scored across with 3 lines.
5. It could be broken into 3 pieces.

B. Join up these half sentences

On the other side	a few hundred years ago.
It could be broken	and spend the lot.
They could be rash	became known as a 'hog'.
It came into use	in half or into quarters.
The coin	was a picture of a pig.

C. Sort out these jumbled words

inco   demlid   rutareq   sharpe   howel

D. Words and phrases

1. What other name was used for a shilling before decimal money came in ?
2. Make a list of names of other coins which were in use before decimal money came in.
3. Write a sentence which includes the phrase *the whole hog*.
4. Think of a well-known phrase which includes one of these words:

pig   **half**   **spend**   **head**

On reflection....

Some years ago, a painting by the famous French artist, Manet, was sent to the U.S.A. for an exhibition. It was shown in the New York Museum of Modern Art. The exhibition ran from April to October.

The painting showed a village reflected in a small lake. After the exhibition was over, the painting was taken down to send back to France. One of the attendants who took it down discovered that it had been hung upside down. No one had noticed !

A. Answer these questions

This is an Australian painting

1. Who was the painter of the picture ?
2. Which country was he from ?
3. In which city was the exhibition held ?
4. Where in that city was the exhibition held ?
5. How long did the exhibition last ?
6. Who discovered that the painting was upside down ?
7. What was shown in the painting ?
8. Where was the painting returned to ?

B. Fill in the right word

1. The painting was by the famous French artist, _____ .
    (Monet / Menet / Manet)
2. It was sent to the U.S.A. for an _____ .
    (exhibit / exhibiting / exhibition)
3. The painting _____ a village and a small lake.
    (showed / shows / show)
4. The painting was of a village _____ in a small lake.
    (reflecting / reflected / reflection)
5. One of the attendants _____ it was upside down.
    (discovers / discovery / discovered)

C. Words within words

How many words are hidden within each of these words ?
e.g. *The word **bit** is hidden in **exhibition***

painting   **attendants**   **discovered**

No suit for a lawyer

A London lawyer arranged to meet some friends for a drink after work. They were meeting because it was the birthday of one of the friends. The lawyer went to the Islington pub straight from work.

When he got there, the barman refused to serve him because he was wearing a suit. The lawyer offered to take off his tie but he was told this wouldn't make any difference. The pub had a policy which stated that customers must not wear 'office attire'. The reason for this was that, in the past, people wearing suits had caused trouble.

Local laws do vary across the U.K. but, in general, pub landlords can refuse to serve anyone they choose.

A. True / False / Maybe

1. The lawyer was meeting some friends.
2. It was the lawyer's birthday.
3. They were meeting in a London pub.
4. The barman was wearing a tie.
5. People wearing suits always cause trouble.

> **PLEASE NOTE**
> This bar is now operating a **NO OFFICE ATTIRE POLICY**

B. Sort out these jumbled sentences

1. friends lawyer to some a arranged meet.
2. birthday it of of the the friends one was.
3. refused the serve to him barman.
4. people had trouble suits caused wearing.
5. landlords refuse they serve to pub anyone choose can.

C. Same spelling - different meaning

Put each of these words into a sentence which gives it a different meaning from the one in the article.

suit   tie   straight   refuse   office

D. What do you think ?

1. If the lawyer had been a woman wearing a suit, would the barman have refused to serve her ?
2. Should pubs be allowed to refuse to serve anyone they choose ?
3. What sort of people make trouble in pubs ?

The first slot machine

Slot machines are everywhere. They can be found in car parks, offices, shops, amusement arcades, phone boxes, and many other public places. You might think that they were invented in the last 100 years. But you would be wrong.

The first slot machine was invented by a Greek man called Hero. He lived in the 1st Century A.D. His slot machine was invented for selling holy water in temples. The water was kept in large urns. Each urn had a pipe coming out of the bottom. A plug closed off the pipe inside the urn. A rod was connected to the plug. When a coin was dropped in a slot near the end of the rod, it tipped the rod down and water came out.

A. Yes / No / Maybe

1. The slot machine was invented about 2000 years ago.
2. The inventor was a hero.
3. The inventor was from Greece.
4. Holy wine was sold from the first slot machine.
5. Amusement arcades were invented in the last 100 years.

B. Which word is the odd one out ?

1. plug   pipe   water   park
2. tipped   bottom   coming   selling
3. slot   rod   urn   shops
4. temples   machine   years   offices

C. Fill in the missing word

1. Slot machines everywhere.
2. The water was kept large urns.
3. A plug closed the pipe inside the urn.
4. A rod connected to the plug.

D. Reading carefully

1. *Make a list of all the words in the article which contain the letter **h**.*

2. *Re-read the description of the first slot machine, then draw a diagram of it.*

E. Beginnings and Endings

1. *Find a word in the article which begins with the same spelling pattern as each of these words:*

   play   **clock**   **slip**   **drink**   **write**   **thank**

2. *Find a word in the article which rhymes with each of these words:*

   round   **bar**   **cases**   **site**   **learns**   **humming**   **beer**

The eagle's eye

Someone who has very good sight is said to be 'eagle-eyed'. But to have eyes as sharp as an eagle's would really be quite something.

Like other birds of prey, eagles have a very wide range of vision. What makes them special is their inner eye. It works in much the same way as a telephoto lens on a camera. The centre of what an eagle sees is magnified to about twice normal size. This means that eagles can spot animals like hares or rabbits very easily. No wonder the eagle is so good at catching its prey.

A. True / False / Maybe

1. Eagles have excellent eyesight.

2. Eagles are birds of prey.

3. Eagles can see a long way.

4. Eagles' eyes are twice as big as human eyes.

5. Eagles eat hares and rabbits.

6. Eagles always catch their prey.

B. Which word is the odd one out ?

1.	animal	hare	eye	rabbit
2.	camera	centre	can	catching
3.	eagle	really	sees	easily
4.	wide	same	size	like

C. Opposites

Find a word in the article which means the opposite of each of these:

bad   narrow   outer

different   made smaller

D. Sort out these jumbled sentences

1. very range of wide eagles have a vision.

2. eye is them inner what their special makes.

3. spot or can eagles easily rabbits very hares.

4. the good prey at its catching is eagle.

E. Phrases

*The phrase **as good as** is used in the article.*

Think of other phrases with the same pattern.

e.g. as cold as   as bright as

F. Word game

Make a list of words containing two or more letters, using the letters in:

telephoto

Index

The index below acts as a rough guide to the main topics covered in the worksheets.

Brown and Brown / Basic Comprehension